The VORDTRIEDE QUIZ

Jürgen Lang

The VORDTRIEDE QUIZ

50 questions and answers
about the emigrated Freiburg family

Some bibliographic information of the German National Library:
The German National Library registers this publication in the German National Bibliography: specified bibliographic data are retrievable on the internet about http://dnb.dnb.de.

© 2016 Jürgen Lang, Fichtestraße 4, 79115 Freiburg

First Edition

All rights reserved. This book or any portion thereof may not be reproduced or used in any manner whatsoever, without the express written permission of the publisher, except for the use of brief quotations in a book review.

Illustration: © 2016 Deutsches Literaturarchiv Marbach
Translation: Jürgen Lang
Other auxiliaries: None

Production and publishing company: BoD - Books on Demand, Norderstedt

ISBN: 978-3-7392-1764-2

Contents

Preface	3
Introduction	5
The VORDTRIEDE HOUSE Freiburg	7
Questions to the project	9
Questions to the dwelling house	11
Questions to Käthe Vordtriede	13
Questions to Fränze Vordtriede	15
Questions to Werner Vordtriede	17
Solution to the quiz	19
Conclusion	21
Index	23
References and biography	25
On the author	35

Preface

The unique quiz informs playfully about the former Jewish family. They lived from 1926 to 1939 in Freiburg Haslach. Behind it there stand single mother Käthe and their children Fränze and Werner. Only because they were Jews, they were pursued and expelled. Through immediate escaping abroad, they could save themselves.

The civic project „The VORDTRIEDE HOUSE Freiburg", would like to remind kindly. Since 2002 the initiator lives with her family in the former dwelling house on Fichte Street 4. In 2015 the private initiative won a City Award for „Civic Engagement".

The target groups of the quiz are adults, young people and kids. Just young people are asked to deal with the German National Socialism and their ideology. These events may never recur, neither here in Freiburg nor somewhere else in the world.

Freiburg im Breisgau, February 2016

The project manager

Introduction

The quiz was developed especially as a contribution to the „Haslacher Adventskalender". On the 15th of December 2015, it was presented to the public for the first time.

The starting point of the idea of creating a quiz was in September 2015, after the Germany-wide article series to the „30th day of death Werner Vordtriede", unfortunately not found resonance.

This booklet wants to wake up interest for the family saga, as well as related subject areas such as emigration, German studies, intellectuals, Jewish history or German National Socialism.

Of course the booklet may be also used as a teaching preparation.

This English first edition corresponds to the German 2nd edition. Merely question No 9 and 35 have been updated and also the references complemented.

The VORDTRIEDE HOUSE Freiburg

The VORDTRIEDE HOUSE is a private initiative which works in the interest of the emigrated family Vordtriede. They lived from 1926 to 1939 at number 4 of the Fichte Street in Freiburg Haslach. Beside Käthe Vordtriede, the children Dr Frances Vordtriede Riley and Prof Werner Vordtriede also belong to it. In 2015 the project won an award for "Civic Engagement".

Initiator is the tenant Jürgen Lang who founded the project in 2014. In the future the former dwelling house could become a meeting place and museum.

There is still a lot to do, by gathering and evaluating of information or perhaps connecting to new contents. Who were the parents Blumenthal for example? What do we know about husband Gustav Adolf Vordtriede? How did Käthe live in New York? What made Fränze in Philadelhia or Werner exactly in Munich? Are there new sources of information?

Consequently the motto of the project is: Recollection, research, reminder.

Should you have something or know on the theme, please turn to the author. Thank you very much.

Questions to the project

1.) When was the project initiated?
        a) 2002
        b) 2004
        c) 2006
        d) 2014

2.) What was the motivation?
        a) 20th day of death Fränze Vordtriede
        b) 30th day of death Werner Vordtriede
        c) 50th day of death Käthe Vordtriede
        d) Centenary of Freiburg Gartenstadt

3.) What could be the motto of the project?
        a) Unity, justice and freedom
        b) Recollection, research, reminder
        c) In vino veritas
        d) Liberté, Egalité, Fraternité ou la mort

4.) What would like to be still the project?
        a) Contact person for the family saga
        b) Contact person for gender equality
        c) Contact person for border crosser
        d) Contact person for schools

5.) Who got the ball rolling?
        a) Biographer dr Gesa Schönermark
        b) Editor Manfred Bosch
        c) Editor Prof Detlef Garz
        d) Scientist Prof Dieter Borchmeyer

6.) Which street name was suggested for the new building area Freiburg Gutleutmatten in 2014?
    a) Dr Vordtriede Riley Blvd
    b) Kaethe Vordtriede Way
    c) Sibs Vordtriede St
    d) W. Vordtriede Ave

7.) Which activities were there in 2015?
    a) 30th day of death Werner Vordtriede
    b) Memorial plaque
    c) Award nominations
    d) Sports day

8.) Which award has the project already got?
    a) Echt gut!-Volunteer work in Baden-Wuerttemberg
    b) Media Prize Bambi
    c) German Civic Prize
    d) City Award for Civic Engagement

9.) What does the year 2016 bring for the project?
    a) Exhibition participation
    b) Membership Freiburg Madison Society
    c) The 900th Birthday of City Freiburg
    d) Wikipedia entries

10.) Which long-term goals does the project have?
    a) Meeting place
    b) Hotel Mom
    c) Museum
    d) Corner Shop

Questions to the dwelling house

11.) Who has pointed out the project manager to the dwelling house?
        a) Colleague
        b) Neighbour
        c) Culture association
        d) City of Freiburg

12.) When did the family move in the dwelling house?
        a) 1918
        b) 1921
        c) 1926
        d) 1933

13.) What did the dwelling house embody at that time?
        a) Welfare work or Erholungsfürsorge
        b) Neighbourly help
        c) Meeting of SPD party members
        d) People´s Guard or Volkswacht

14.) In which epochs did the Vordtriede´s live?
        a) Berliner Republic
        b) German Empire
        c) Third Reich
        d) Weimar Republic

15.) Why were they pursued and expelled?
        a) Emigrants
        b) Intellectuals
        c) Jews
        d) Westphalians

16.) How many inhabitants had Freiburg in 1939 when the house was left?
- a) 99,122
- b) 108,487
- c) 116,731
- d) 222,203

17.) What did Werner Vordtriede say to a neighbour when he visited the former dwelling house?
- a) I am a Berliner!
- b) I am looking for the city!
- c) I search my youth!
- d) I know that I know nothing!

18.) Who of the family Vordtriede visited the dwelling house at last?
- a) Frances Vordtriede Riley
- b) Julius Vordtriede
- c) Käthe Vordtriede
- d) Werner Vordtriede

19.) When did it come to the Stumble Stone laying in front of the house?
- a) 1996
- b) 1999
- c) 2004
- d) 2006

20.) Who owns the dwelling house today?
- a) Building Society or Bauverein Breisgau
- b) German Foundation for Monument Protection
- c) The Family Alber Lang
- d) Housing Association or Stadtbau Freiburg

Questions to Käthe Vordtriede

21.) Where was she born?
      a) Bielefeld
      b) Freiburg
      c) Hanover
      d) Karlsruhe

22.) What was the profession of husband Gustav Adolf Vordtriede?
      a) Bank clerk
      b) Mayor
      c) Craftsman
      d) Manufacturer for chocolate

23.) What did Käthe work mainly in Freiburg?
      a) Housewife
      b) Political journalist
      c) Postal employee
      d) Authoress

24.) Which drastic live events were there in 1933?
      a) Professional ban
      b) Emigration of son Werner
      c) Arresting
      d) Destruction of the Volkswacht printery

25.) How did she become known all over Germany?
      a) Book publication
      b) Television series
      c) Celebrity wedding
      d) News article

26.) How is her first publication called?
    a) The Seventh Cross (1942)
    b) The Lost House (1975)
    c) It is still like a dream for me, if I managed this adventurous escape (1998)
    d) Telemachs Transfiguration (1995)

27.) Which year was the Kaethe Vordtriede Way suggested for the first time?
    a) 1999
    b) 2000
    c) 2002
    d) 2014

28.) Where is the second Stumble Stone of Käthe Vordtriede?
    a) Freiburg (Basle Court)
    b) Hanover
    c) Kreuzlingen (Switzerland)
    d) Lengwil (Switzerland)

29.) What did she work finally?
    a) Journalist
    b) Housekeeper
    c) Woman teacher
    d) Authoress of novels

30.) When did Käthe Vordtriede die?
    a) 1939 in Frauenfeld (Switzerland)
    b) 1961 in Muinch
    c) 1964 in New York City
    d) 1994 in Freiburg

Questions to Fränze Vordtriede

31.) Where was she born?
    a) Bielefeld
    b) Dortmund
    c) Munich
    d) New York City

32.) How was Fränze involved in her spare time?
    a) Band of German Maidens
    b) Welfare work with the mother
    c) Youth movement Wandervogel
    d) Aid organization for winter

33.) Where did she make her high school diploma?
    a) Berthold State Gymnasium
    b) Friedrich State Gymnasium
    c) Goethe State Gymnasium
    d) Kepler State Gymnasium

34.) What has Fränze studied in Freiburg?
    a) Anglistics
    b) Medical study
    c) Law
    d) Ecomonics

35.) How old was she at the doctoral thesis with Prof Friedrich Brie?
    a) 19-year-old
    b) 24-year-old
    c) 28-year-old
    d) 32-year-old

36.) In which country did Fränze emigrate in 1934?
    a) France
    b) Great Britain
    c) Switzerland
    d) USA

37.) Where did she live after her marriage with the colleague William Thomas Riley in 1951?
    a) Harrisburgh
    b) New York City
    c) Philadelphia
    d) Woodstock

38.) Which profession did Frances practice at last?
    a) Kindergartener
    b) Woman teacher
    c) Administration sectretary
    d) Research assistant

39.) When has „Fränzi" died?
    a) 1961 in Munich
    b) 1964 in New York City
    c) 1994 in Freiburg
    d) 1997 in Fort Myers

40.) Which title does an essay have about her?
    a) A politically dangerous subject (2002)
    b) There are times in those one wilts (1999)
    c) Secrets at the Lummer (1979)
    d) Weimar on the Pacific (1985)

Questions to Werner Vordtriede

41.) Where was Werner born?
        a) Bielefeld
        b) Dortmund
        c) Hanover
        d) Munich

42.) In which country did the high school graduate emigrate and did study there later?
        a) Great Britain
        b) Italy
        c) Switzerland
        d) USA

43.) In which well-known university did he become a professor at the age of only 32 years?
        a) Albert Ludwig´s University in 1955
        b) Ludwig Maximilian´s University in 1962
        c) University of Zurich in 1943
        d) University of Wisconsin in 1947

44.) When did Werner go back to Germany?
        a) 1945
        b) 1961
        c) 1963
        d) 1985

45.) What did he make professional?
        a) Poet
        b) Literary scholar
        c) Author
        d) Translator

46.) What was his first publication?
- a) The Lost House (1975)
- b) The Deep Thinker (1981)
- c) The Necromancer (1968)
- d) Amorous poetry (1980)

47.) For which Nobel Prize Laureate of Literature had he published poems in 1963?
- a) Frédéric Mistral (France)
- b) George Bernhard Shaw (Great Britain)
- c) Pearl S. Buck (USA)
- d) William Butler Yeats (Irland)

48.) Where did he live in Munich?
- a) Kunigunde Street No 35
- b) Marys Place No 11
- c) Sendling Gate
- d) Simmern Street No 3

49.) When did the „Homme de lettres" die?
- a) 1980 in Bielefeld
- b) 1982 in Freiburg
- c) 1985 in Smyrna/Izmir (Turkey)
- d) 1998 in New York City

50.) Who is managing all estate records?
- a) Schiller Society or Schiller Gesellschaft
- b) German Literary Archive
- c) Alum
- d) UW-Madison Libraries

Solution to the quiz

<u>To the project</u>: **1d**, **2c**, **3b**, **4a/d**, **5b**, **6c**, **7a/c**, **8d**, **9a/b/d** and **10a/c**.

<u>To the dwelling house</u>: **11b**, **12c**, **13a-d**, **14c/d**, **15b/c**, **16b**, **17c**, **18a**, **19d** and **20a**.

<u>To Käthe Vordtriede</u>: **21c**, **22d**, **23b**, **24a-d**, **25a**, **26c**, **27b**, **28a**, **29b** and **30c**.

<u>To Fränze Vordtriede</u>: **31b**, **32b/c**, **33c**, **34a**, **35b**, **36b**, **37c**, **38b**, **39d** and **40a**.

<u>To Werner Vordtriede</u>: **41a**, **42c/d**, **43d**, **44b**, **45a-d**, **46a**, **47d**, **48a/d**, **49c** and **50b**.

Conclusion

The Quiz has given first insight into the family history and maybe has aroused further interest.

Beside Käthe Vordtriede the children Fränze and Werner were also considered. All three of them were victims of the Nazis´ race mania.

Finally a context was produced with the questions between Nazi era, places, people, project and the former dwelling house. An interesting general view and other questions arise from it.

Partly new facts were used.

Extensive list of references and biography can be used for more information or reading tips.

Index

Aktionskomitee 100 Jahre Gartenstadt, 27
Award for Civic Engagement, 3, 10
Band of German Maidens, 15
Bielefeld, 17
Building society or Bauverein Breisgau, 12, 27
Centenary of Freiburg Gartenstadt, 9
Dortmund, 15
Dr Frances Vordtriede Riley, 7, 12
Dr Gesa Schönermark, 9, 30
Dr Sigrun Faltin, 28
Dr Ute Scherb, 27
Echt Gut!-Volunteer work in Baden Wurttemberg, 10
Emigration, 31
Fichte Street, 3, 7
50th day of death Käthe Vordtriede, 9
Fort Myers, 17
Fränze Vordtriede, 3, 15, 16, 26, 27
Frauenfeld, 14
Freiburg, 3, 10, 12, 14
German Civic Prize, 10
German Literary Archive, 18
German National Socialism, 3, 21, 33, 34
German Philology, 32
Goethe State Gymnasium, 15
Great Britain, 16
Gustav Adolf Vordtriede, 7, 13
Hanover, 13
Intellectuals, 11, 32
Jews, 3, 11
Jews history, 32
Jürgen Lang, 7, 25, 26, 28, 30, 35

Julius Vordtriede, 12
Käthe Vordtriede, 3, 7, 13, 14, 27, 28, 29
Kaethe Vordtriede Way, 14
Kunigunde Street, 18
Ludwigs Maximilian's University, 17
Manfred Bosch, 9, 28
Munich, 7, 18
New York City, 7, 14
Parents Blumenthal, 7
People's Guard or *Volkswacht*, 11, 13
Philadelphia, 7, 16
Prof Detlef Garz, 9, 28
Prof Dieter Borchmeyer, 9, 29
Prof Friedrich Brie, 15
Sibs Vordtriede St, 10
Simmern Street, 18
Smyrna/Izmir, 18
Stumbling Stones, 12, 14
Switzerland, 14
The Vordtriede House, 3, 7, 25, 26
Third Reich, 11
30th day of death Werner Vordtriede, 5, 10
Thomas William Riley, 16
University of Wisconsin, 17
University of Zurich, 17
USA, 17
Weimar Republic, 11
Welfare work or Erholungsfürsorge, 11, 15
Werner Vordtriede, 3, 7, 17, 18, 29, 30
Westphalians, 11
Wikipedia entries, 10
William Butler Yeats, 18, 30
Woodstock, 16
Youth movement Wandervogel, 15

References and biography

General:

Own study

www.uni-freiburg.de

www.stadt-freiburg.de

www.verwaltungsgeschichte.de

The Vordtriede House:

de.wikipedia.org/wiki/Vordtriede-Haus_Freiburg
(30.01.2016)

Gröber, Bettina
Brückenbauer und Lotsen, Die Stadt hat Ehrenamtliche und Freiwillige für langjähriges Engagement ausgezeichnet, in: Badische Zeitung, Freiburg 04.12.2015

Lang, Jürgen
Am Tisch mit Käthe Vordtriede, Erinnerungen an das großartige Engagement der jüdischen Schriftstellerin, abrufbar unter: www.regiotrends.de, Freiburg am 06.01.2015

Lang, Jürgen
Das VORDTRIEDE-HAUS Freiburg, Mahnmal gegen Gewaltherrschaft und Vergessen, Werbeflyer, Freiburg 2014

Lang, Jürgen
Geschwister-Vordtriede-Straße für Gutleutmatten-West, in: Haslacher Bote, Oktober-Ausgabe, Freiburg 2014

Lang, Jürgen
Projekt VORDTRIEDE-HAUS Freiburg nominiert, Dabei beim Wettbewerb Echt-Gut!-Ehrenamt in Baden-Württemberg 2015, abrufbar unter: www.regiotrends.de, Freiburg am 03.07.2015

Lang, Jürgen
Verloren aber in der Sache gewonnen!, in: Haslacher Bote, Dezember-Ausgabe, Freiburg 2014

Lang, Jürgen
VORDTRIEDE-HAUS Freiburg erhält Auszeichnung, Preisgeld wird für Forschungsarbeiten verwendet, abrufbar unter: www.regiotrends.de, Freiburg am 04.12.2015

Lang, Jürgen
VORDTRIEDE-HAUS Freiburg veröffentlicht Quiz, Ehemaliges Wohnhaus soll Begegnungsstätte und Museum werden, abrufbar unter: www.regiotrends.de, Freiburg am 13.11.2015

Wielsch, Regina
Haslacher Adventskalender 2015, in: Haslacher Bote, November-Ausgabe, Freiburg 2015

Fränze Vordtriede:

Der Imagismus, Sein Wesen und seine Bedeutung, Freiburg 1935

de.wikipedia.org/wiki/Fränze_Vordtriede (12.01.2016)

Own study

Huml, Ariane u.a.
Jüdische Intellektuelle im 20. Jahrhundert, Literatur- und kunstgeschichtliche Studien, Würzburg 2003

Peterfly, Margit
William Carlos Williams in deutscher Sprache, Aspekte der übersetzerischen Übermittlung 1951-1970, Würzburg 1999

Pfanz-Sponagel, Christiane
Als die Heimat zur Fremde wurde. Zwischen Emigration und Deportation, Die Freiburger Juden als Opfer des NS-Rassenwahns, in: Migration in Freiburg im Breisgau, Ihre Geschichte von 1500 bis zur Gegenwart, Freiburg 2014

Scherb, Ute
Ein politisch gefährliches Subjekt, Das Leben der Fränze Vordtriede, in: Zeitschrift des Breigau Geschichtsvereins Schau-ins-Land, 121. Jahresheft, Freiburg 2002

www.ancestry.co.uk

www.dla-marbach.de

Käthe Vordtriede:

Aktionskomitee 100 Jahre Gartenstadt
Die Gestapo durchwühlte gerade unsere Küche, in: Geschichte und Geschichten, 100 Jahre Gartenstadt Freiburg-Haslach, Freiburg 2014

Baureithel, Ulrike
Nun sind wir gar nichts, in: Die Welt, Berlin 06.02.1999

Bauverein Breisgau
Der Bauverein Breisgau in der Gartenstadt, ein Rück- und Ausblick anlässlich ihres 100-jährigen Jubiläums, in: Lebensräume, Juli-Ausgabe, Freiburg 2014

Bochtler, Anja
Auf den Spuren von Käthe Vordtriede, in: Badische Zeitung, Freiburg 09.08.2014

Bosch, Manfred (Hrsg.)
Mir ist es noch wie ein Traum, dass mir diese abenteuerliche Flucht gelang, Briefe nach 1933 aus Freiburg, Frauenfeld und New York an ihren Sohn Werner, Lengwil 1998

de.wikipedia.org/wiki/Käthe_Vordtriede (27.09.2015)

Own study

Faltin, Sigrid
Chronistin in dunkler Zeit, Die Freiburger Journalistin Käthe Vordtriede, Doku-Film, Baden-Baden 2001, abrufbar unter www.youtube.com

Garz, Detlef (Hrsg.)
Es gibt Zeiten, in denen man welkt, Mein Leben in Deutschland vor und nach 1933, Lengwil 1999

Lang, Jürgen
Berühmte Vormieterin, in: Stadtkurier, Freiburg 07.08.2014

Lang, Jürgen
Meine Vormieterin Käthe Vordtriede, Freiburger Jahre der jüdischen Redakteurin und Schriftstellerin, Beitrag zur Festschrift 100 Jahre Gartenstadt, Freiburg 27.03.2014

Lernort Zivilcourage & Widerstand
Randale in der Redaktion, Käthe Vordtriede erlebt die Erstürmung der Freiburger Volkswacht, Kurz-Film, Karlsruhe 2015, abrufbar unter www.youtube.com

Rehm, Sigrun
Raus mit der Marxistenhexe, in: Der Sonntag, Freiburg 10.08.2014

Von Ebel, Martin
Ein Volk von Umfallern, in: Der Spiegel, Ausgabe 44, Hamburg 1999

www.dla-marbach.de

www.freiburgs-geschichte.de/1933-1945

www.juedischeliteraturwestfalen.de

www.kalliope.staatsbibliothek-berlin.de

www.perlentaucher.de/autor/kaethe-vordtriede

www.schule-bw.de/unterricht

<u>Werner Vordtriede</u>:

Bermbach Udo und Vaget Hans R.
Getauft auf Musik, Festschrift für Dieter Borchmeyer, Würzburg 2006

Borchmeyer, Dieter u.a.
Weimar am Pazifik, literarische Wege zwischen den Kontinenten, Festschrift für Werner Vordtriede zum 70. Geburtstag, Berlin 1985

Das verlassene Haus, Tagebuch aus dem amerikanischen Exil 1938-1947, München 1975

Der Innenseiter, Roman, München 1981

de.wikipedia.org/wiki/Werner_Vordtriede (02.08.2015)

Own study

Geheimnisse an der Lummer, Roman, Wien 1979

Hergemöller, Bernd U.
Mann für Mann, Biographisches Lexikon zur Geschichte von Freundesliebe und männlicher Sexualität im deutschen Sprachraum, Münster 2010

König, Christoph
Internationales Germanistenlexikon 1800-1959, Band 1, A-G, Tübingen 2003

Lang, Jürgen
Den bleiben ist nirgens, Erinnerungen zum 30. Todestag des Exilanten Werner Vordtriede, in: Haslacher Bote, Oktober-Ausgabe, Freiburg 2015

Melchinger, Christa
Spiegelromane, Werner Vordtriede: Der Innenseiter und Ulrichs Ulrich, in: Die Zeit, München 10.12.1982

Schönermark, Gesa
Telemachs Wandlung, Werner Vordtriede. Eine wissenshistorische Biografie, München 1995

Ulrichs Ulrich oder Vorbereitungen zum Untergang, München 1985

William Butler Yeats, Liebesgedichte, Neuwied am Rhein 1980

www.ancestry.co.uk

www.dla-marbch.de

www.juedischeliteraturwestfalen.de

www.kalliope.staatsbibliothek-berlin.de

www.literaturportal-westfalen.de

Emigration:

Anderson, Edith
Liebe im Exil, Berlin 2010

Blubacher, Thomas
Paradies in schwerer Zeit, Künstler und Denker im Exil in Pacific Palisades, München 2011

Bollauf, Traude
Dienstmädchen-Emigration, Die Flucht jüdischer Frauen aus Österreich und Deutschland nach England 1938/39, Münster 2011

Emmerich, Alexander
Die Geschichte der Deutschen in Amerika, Von 1860 bis zur Gegenwart, Köln 2013

Feuchtwanger, Lion
Exil, Roman, Berlin 2008

Fischer, Erika
Himmelsstraße, Geschichte meiner Familie, Berlin 2007

Kerr, Judith
Warten bis der Friede kommt, Jugendbuch, Ravensburg 1997

Klapdor, Heike
In der Ferne das Glück, Geschichten für Hollywood, Berlin 2013

Remarque, E. M.
Das gelobte Land, Roman, Köln 2010

Roth, Joseph
Juden auf der Flucht, München 2006

German philology:

Drügh, Heinz u.a.
Germanistik, Sprachenwissenschaft-Literaturwissenschaft-Schlüsselkompetenzen, Stuttgart 2012

Intellectuals:

Burschel, Peter u.a.
Intellektuelle im Exil, Göttingen 2011

Winkler, Michael
Deutsche Literatur im Exil 1933-1945, Texte und Dokumente. Ditzingen 1997

Ziegler, Edda
Verboten-verfemt-vertrieben, Schriftstellerinnen im Widerstand gegen den Nationalsozialismus, München 2010

Jews history:

Ben-Sasson, H. H.
Geschichte des jüdischen Volkes, Von den Anfängen bis zur Gegenwart, München 2007

Herzig, Arno
Jüdische Geschichte in Deutschland, Von den Anfängen bis zur Gegenwart, München, 2002

Jüdisches Museum Berlin
Zweitausend Jahre deutsch-jüdische Geschichte, Köln 2002

Steinecke, Hartmut u.a.
Jüdisches Kulturerbe in Westfalen, Spurensuche zu jüdischer Kultur in Vergangenheit und Gegenwart, Bielefeld 2009

German National Socialism:

Anne Frank Fond, Basel (Hrsg.)
Anne Frank Gesamtausgabe, Tagebücher, Geschichte und Ereignisse aus dem Hinterhaus, Erzählungen, Briefe, Fotos und Dokumente, Frankfurt am Main 2015

Benz, Wolfgang
Das Tagebuch der Hertha Nathorff, Berlin-New York, Tagebuchaufzeichnungen 1933 bis 1945, Frankfurt am Main 1989

Jens, Inge (Hrsg.)
Hans Scholl und Sophie Scholl, Briefe und Aufzeichnungen, Frankfurt am Main 1988

Knopp, Guido
Hitlers Helfer, München 1998

Longerich, Peter
Davon haben wir nichts gewusst!, Die Deutschen und die Judenverfolgung 1933-1945, München 2007

Meckel, Marlies
Den Opfern ihre Namen zurückgeben, Stolpersteine in Freiburg, Freiburg 2006

Nürnberger, Christian
Mutige Menschen, Widerstand im Dritten Reich, Stuttgart 2015

Rees, Laurence
Auschwitz, Geschichte eines Verbrechens, Leipzig 2007

Seghers, Anna
Das siebte Kreuz, Berlin 1995

Stadtarchiv Freiburg
Das Schicksal der Freiburger Juden am Beispiel des Kaufmanns Max Mayer und die Ereignisse des 9./10. November 1938, Freiburg 2000

Zielke-Nadkarni, Andrea u.a.
Man sieht nur, was man weiß, NS-Verfolgte im Alter, Fallgeschichten und Lernmaterial, Frankfurt am Main 2013

Zweig, Stefanie
Die Kinder der Rothschildallee, Band 2 der Rothschild-Saga, Roman, München 2010

On the author

The bank clerk and graduate in business management Jürgen Lang acts for over 30 years in the finance branch. It is his vocation. His favorite subjects are stock exchange and investment. Further he is interested in analyses, globalization and leadership. Present activities were branch manager, financial advisor, security advisor, customer advisor and stand-in. He lives and works as a professional analyst, author and coach in the Green City Freiburg.

His books are available in book shops, web stores and several publishers. In 2014 he published audio books about the BRICS countries Brazil, Russia, India, China and South Africa. His first narrative and biography followed in 2015, as well as the third book series on the topic of shares.

You can reach the author under the email address juergenlang63@gmx.de.